Jamaica

by Ali Brownlie

WATERBIRD BOOKS

Columbus, Ohio

Other Titles in This Series:

Canada   France   Italy

 Children's Publishing

This edition published in the United State of America in 2003 by
Waterbird Books
an imprint of McGraw-Hill Children's Publishing,
a Division of The McGraw-Hill Companies
8787 Orion Place
Columbus, Ohio 43240-4027

www.MHkids.com

Library of Congress Cataloging-in-Publication Data is on file with the publisher.

© Hodder Wayland 2003

Hodder Wayland is an imprint of Hodder Children's Books

Printed in China.

1-57768-877-5

1 2 3 4 5 6 7 8 9 10 HOD 09 08 07 06 05 04 03

Contents

Where Is Jamaica?

Jamaica is the third largest island in the Caribbean Sea. Almost three million people live there. Its capital city is Kingston.

Many people visit the tropical island of Jamaica every year.

People come from all over the world to live in Jamaica. That is why there is such a mixture of music, food, and religions.

4

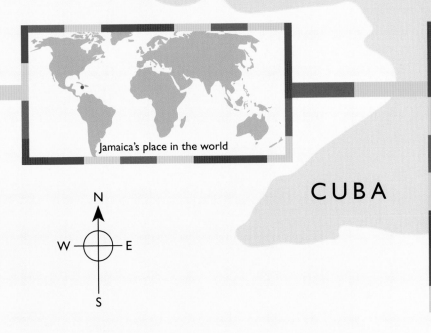

Jamaica's place in the world

JAMAICA FACTS

Jamaica is 146 miles long and 50 miles wide.

Most Jamaicans live in the towns of Kingston, Montego Bay, Spanish Town, and Mandeville.

Arawak Indians named the island *Jamaica,* meaning "land of wood and water."

CUBA

N
W — E
S

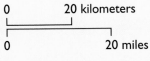

0   20 kilometers

0   20 miles

C A R I B B E A N   S E A

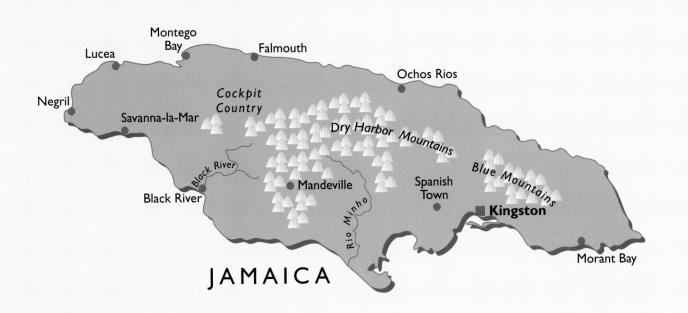

Montego Bay
Lucea
Falmouth
Negril
Ochos Rios
Savanna-la-Mar
Cockpit Country
Dry Harbor Mountains
Black River
Blue Mountains
Black River
Mandeville
Spanish Town
Rio Minho
Kingston
Morant Bay

JAMAICA

5

Cities

Kingston is the largest city in Jamaica. Almost 750,000 people live there. Many people from the countryside go to Kingston to look for work. Kingston has banks, office buildings, and shopping malls. ▼

Kingston Harbor is so large that people ride a ferry from one side to the other.

Montego Bay, on the northwest coast, is the second largest city in Jamaica. It has hotels and sandy beaches.

This plane landing at Montego Bay is bringing more **tourists** to Jamaica.

The Landscape

Most of Jamaica is mountainous. The mountains are covered by thick forests and surrounded by flat, coastal **plains**. Rivers form waterfalls as they tumble down the mountain slopes.

Coffee beans grown in the Blue Mountains are used to make coffee all over the world.

Jamaica is surrounded by the warm, clear water of the Caribbean Sea. The island has some of the most famous beaches in the world.

On the west coast, there are **coral reefs** in the shallow ocean water.

The Weather

The Jamaican coasts are hot and **humid** all year round. However, the north coast gets more rain than the south. The weather is also cooler in the mountains.

Trees shade this Jamaican river from the hot sun.

◀

Strong winds and heavy rainfall can damage houses and cause **landslides** and floods.

Between May and November, **tropical storms** and **hurricanes** can occur in Jamaica. During these months, fewer tourists visit.

11

Transportation

In Jamaica, most people travel by small buses, which go all over the island. Children who live in **remote** areas walk or ride a bus to school.

Buses leave when they are full. They do not follow a schedule.

More and more people own cars in Jamaica. The roads and cities are getting busier.

Traffic jams are common in large cities like Kingston.

Farming

Many Jamaicans are farmers. Some farmers work on **plantations** growing coffee, **sugar cane,** and bananas. These crops are usually sold to other countries.

Coffee beans are washed, roasted, and then packed.

Other farmers run their own small farms. They grow fruit and vegetables for their own use, or they sell them in local markets.

Many types of fruits and vegetables are grown in Jamaica.

15

Food

Jamaican food is rich and spicy. The national dish is salt fish and a fruit called *ackee*. When cooked, ackee tastes a little like scrambled eggs.

Salt fish and ackee are often eaten with plantains, fruits shaped like bananas.

Other traditional dishes are pepperpot soup, curried goat, rice, beans, chicken, and brown fish stew. Jamaicans are also known for using **jerk**, a hot spice, in their cooking.

These children are eating rice, chicken, and fish at the beach.

17

Shopping

In cities, there are supermarkets that sell a large range of products. On the streets, women called *higglers* sell homegrown fruit and vegetables.

Many smaller shops are found in Jamaica's shopping malls.

In country villages, there may be only one shop. That shop will usually sell all of the basic things that people need.

▼

This man is selling pineapples and other tropical fruit.

At Work

Many people in Jamaica work in the tourist industry. Some people work in hotels and bars or as tour guides.

Many Jamaicans earn money by making **souvenirs** for tourists.

The bauxite industry **employs** Jamaicans as well. Bauxite is a valuable metal mined on the island. It is used to make tin cans.

Bauxite is sometimes known as "red gold."

Having Fun

Most Jamaicans love music. The beat of Jamaican music, known as **reggae music**, can be heard all over the island.

This is a statue of Bob Marley. His music made reggae popular all over the world.

Jamaicans play sports, such as soccer, cricket, basketball, and baseball. Young people also spend much of their time playing computer games at home.

Soccer is one of the most popular sports in Jamaica.

Festivals

Most people in Jamaica are Christians. On Christian holidays like Easter or Christmas, everyone wears their best clothes. There are dances and processions in the streets.

Many Jamaicans attend church regularly.

On Independence Day, people parade through Kingston wearing colorful costumes.

Independence Day is on August 6th. On this day, a big parade moves through the streets of Kingston to the National Stadium. There, everyone celebrates with music and dancing.

Jamaican Scrapbook

This is a scrapbook of some everyday things you might find in Jamaica.

An advertisement for a gift shop in Montego Bay.

A postcard of the northeast coast of Jamaica.

Jamaicans use Jamaican dollars and cents. There are 100 cents in a dollar.

28

A children's comic book.

An entry ticket for the Bob Marley Museum in Kingston.

Phonecards like these can be used to place calls in Jamaica.

Glossary

Coral reef The hard skeletons of tiny sea animals found underwater in large, colorful groups.

Employ To give people jobs and a salary.

Humid When the air holds a large amount of water vapor.

Hurricane A storm with very strong and damaging winds.

Jerk A hot Jamaican spice used in cooking.

Landslide When soil becomes so wet that it slips down a hillside.

Plain A flat area of land.

Plantation A large area where crops are planted.

Reggae music A simple, lively, and rhythmic form of music found in Jamaica.

Remote A place that is far from other towns and cities.

Shanty town A town with many makeshift houses.

Souvenir A thing that is kept as a reminder of a place, person, or event.

Sugar cane The plant used to make sugar.

Tourist A person who is visiting a place during a vacation.

Tropical storm A small, violent storm in the Caribbean Sea.

Further Information

Some Jamaican Words

a-doors	outside
aringe	orange
bafan	clumsy
beenie	small
darkers	sunglasses
labrish	gossip
nuff	plenty
pickney	child
smadi	somebody
wamek	why
yahso	here

Further Reading From McGraw-Hill Children's Publishing

What's It Like to Live in Italy? (ISBN 1-57768-876-7)

What's It Like to Live in France? (ISBN 1-57768-875-9)

What's It Like to Live in Canada? (ISBN 1-57768-878-3)

Index